MW01199593

How To Celebrate Passover
© Copyright 2004

Published by Master Press
8905 Kingston Pike #316 Knoxville, TN 37923
Master Press Website: www.master-press.com
1-800-325-9136

Distributed by Master Press

ISBN: 0-9646543-9-3
All rights reserved

No part of this book may be reproduced or transmitted in any form or by any means, electronic, mechanical, including photocopying, recording, or by any information storage and retrieval system, without permission in writing from the publisher.

Printed in the United States of America

How To Celebrate
פסח
Passover

"A Practical Guide For Christians"
(Complete with Haggadah)

W. Charles Greenfield

Published by Master Press

פסח INDEX

FOREWORD

פסח

The Jewish Perspective on Passover

by Neil Silverberg

Throughout the worldwide church there has been a growing interest for many years in the ancient Jewish feast of Passover, and in particular the Seder, the celebratory meal that commemorates its beginnings. More and more Christians are showing an interest in conducting Jewish Seders both in their own homes and churches. Each Passover season it is common to find Jewish believers leading Passover Seder presentations in many churches throughout the land.

Why all this interest in the Passover and in particular the Seder meal? Some have dismissed it as mere Gentile fascination with ancient Judaism. Yet closer inspection will reveal that there is clearly more to this phenomenon. It is rooted in the fact that believers are beginning to recognize that the roots of their own faith extend deeply into the Hebrew Bible (Old Testament) and are intimately related to the history of the Jewish people. This realization has spawned intense interest in understanding such things as the feasts of Israel, those appointed times God commanded Israel to keep in celebration of the covenant. Obviously this has brought the Passover front and center, since it was the first and greatest of Israel's covenantal celebrations.

For the church, the Passover Seder meal should have special significance since her own celebration of Communion is a carryover from it. Much of the New Testament's description of redemption is drawn largely from the Passover motif. Jesus is God's Lamb whose blood is applied to the hearts and consciences of believers. The elements of the Lord's Supper, bread and wine, are drawn largely from the Passover Seder meal. The Christian therefore has more than a passing interest in this ancient feast and its traditional meal on the first night.

For over twenty years I have personally seen first-hand the benefit of helping Christians to understand the Jewish Seder. Each year I conduct Seder meal demonstrations in churches throughout North America. My particular presentation focuses on recreating all of the events which transpired between Jesus and the disciples in the Upper Room during the Last Supper. Many believers are not even aware that the Last Supper was indeed a Seder meal Messiah held with His twelve closest friends on earth. Seeing the events of that evening in the context of the Jewish Seder powerfully demonstrates how the Lord took the elements of the traditional Seder and gave them new meaning. Each time I present it Christians testify to an entire new understanding of the Lord's Supper they had not previously known.

As the desire to understand Passover has grown, so naturally has the desire to celebrate the Seder. Unfortunately there has been a dearth of practical materials designed to assist believers in the conducting of the Seder. That is why I am pleased to commend Chas Greenfield's new work, How To Celebrate The Passover to the church at large. Pastor Greenfield has taken all of the hard work out of holding a Seder by writing a practical hands-on guide which any believer or church can follow. Each page is full of practical instruction dealing with such things as the proper prayers, the preparation of food, and other practical aspects of the Seder. This welcome guide is just the thing needed for believers and churches who, though interested in conducting a Seder, have up to now been intimated for lack of knowledge.

My hope is that this Haggadah, the traditional name for the book guiding worshippers through the Seder celebration, will encourage more and more churches to celebrate the Passover. The goal should not be for the church simply to become more Jewish but to discover her own roots in the covenant of Israel, as well as the relationship between the old and new covenants. To that end, Pastor Greenfield's contribution will go a long way in accomplishing that. That is why I heartily recommend it for any believer or church ready to take the plunge and "keep the Festival" (I Corinthians 5:8 New International Version).

INTRODUCTION

פסח

THE HEART AND PLACE OF CHRISTIANS IN THE PASSOVER

The wonder and amazement of Passover has been celebrated for centuries by the remnant of Israel. Yet, today, many Christians have a growing hunger to enjoy this timeless festival as well. However, many Christians are confused when it comes to understanding their place in the Jewish feasts, festivals, and traditions. Persons interested in learning more about the feasts, and actually celebrating the Passover, are often concerned that their fellow believers might misinterpret their actions. They are worried that they will be considered weird or even cultic. And, of course, there is always the concern that the Jewish community, itself, might not understand a believer's decision to celebrate the Passover. So making the decision to celebrate Passover can be quite complex.

Even when a Christian family takes this giant step to celebrate the Passover, they often find a complete lack of information on how to do so. Or else, they lack the appropriate understanding to put all the pieces together. This book has been especially prepared to give a Christian family the information necessary to practically prepare and enjoy a Passover Seder, as well as understand what is involved.

Does a Christian have a seat at the Passover table? Is it appropriate for Christians to celebrate the Passover? Undoubtedly, the answer is yes! Non-Jewish individuals who feared God and showed reverence to Him were always given a place within Jewish society as a whole. Regarding the Passover, God prepared a place for the non-Jew at the table from the very beginning. In fact, when the laws concerning the Passover were given to Moses, Israel was commanded to include the visiting outsider (see Numbers 9:14). Yet how should a Christian today approach Passover? The first thing we must do is, acknowledge that the Passover is a Jewish celebration. The Passover was given to Israel, and it is for Israel. The Jewish people celebrate Passover by commandment as an obligatory service and a privilege. They are under a mandate from God to celebrate Passover until time itself ends. For the Jew, celebrating Passover is not an option. By contrast, the non-Jewish believer in Y'shua (Jesus) is invited to enjoy the celebration as a guest, free from obligation. Yet, as a guest, our approach must be one of respect and submission. We show honor to those who have conducted themselves in the traditions of Passover for thousands of years. When we conduct our own Passover celebrations, we adhere to their standards, acknowledging their role in our actions. Our approach is one of humility, not arrogance. We see ourselves as joined celebrants of a timeless feast.

The sense of belonging and being a part of a larger community is a foundational reality for the Jewish faith. Celebrating the Passover creates a bond between us and the Jewish heritage, which is the foundation for our Christian faith. We identify with those who have gone before us. We thank God for those who have paid a price for the faith we now enjoy. By keeping the Passover, we personally identify with those who were dramatically freed from the yoke of slavery in Egypt. Yet for the believer in Jesus, there is even more than this.

The actions of the Lord, at His final Passover Seder, and His fulfillment of both the biblical commands regarding the feast and the Jewish traditions, bring anticipation and a hunger to anyone who has bowed their knee to Him. Whether physically born into the Jewish community, or an outsider, we long to see our Savior in the feast. We want to see more and hear more of the wonder and majesty found at Calvary. When we celebrate Passover, we see Jesus, and catch a deeper glimpse of what He has done for us. As we celebrate Passover with the Jewish community, an appreciation and love for the feast begins to grow within our hearts. We find that we are worshiping like we have not done before. We see, with amazement, the complete work done by God for our salvation, deliverance, and redemption.

The fact that more and more Christians are beginning to join the Jewish community in the celebration of Passover is not surprising. We recognize something familiar in the Passover: Communion. The "Communion" is an early church tradition that is an outgrowth of Passover. The reverence, holiness, anticipation, and joy experienced at the Communion table are snapshots of the broader Passover experience. When we celebrate Passover for the first time, we get a more complete taste of what we have been enjoying for years. We begin to appreciate why the Lord instructed His disciples to remember Him by celebrating the Passover after His departure.

So enjoy! The remainder of this book will address the actual evening of Passover and how a Christian may practically join in this timeless feast!

Section One

פסח

The Passover Seder

&

Haggadah

(A Liturgy for the Passover Seder)

פֶּסַח

The Pesach Haggadah is used as a guide for the actual Passover celebration. Once all preparation has been made and all the participants have arrived, this section may be followed as a responsive reading for the evening. If you are interested in further understanding Passover, without actually celebrating the feast, simply read Section One for a glimpse of this timeless event.

See Section Three and the Appendix for how to prepare for the Passover Seder.

Roles to Fill: *Host (father or male head of the house)*
Hostess (wife of the host)
Historian
Interpreter
Adult readers 1 & 2
Child readers 1 & 2
Music Coordinator (someone to operate a tape deck, play an instrument, or lead the singing)

בְּרִיקַת חָמֵץ SEARCHING FOR THE CHAMETZ

Have everyone gather to begin the evening

The Host now searches for a small heap of bread crumbs that the Hostess has left (mercifully) in an obvious place using a napkin and a feather. Once the Leaven has been found, begin.

Historian: Prior to the Passover celebration, the house has been thoroughly cleaned and all products containing yeast have been removed. Historically, the head of the house inspects the home to insure that the Passover requirement has been met. He searches the home with a feather and napkin for a small portion of leaven that his wife has left for him to find. Once the leaven has been found, he brushes it into the napkin, folds the napkin, and recites the following just prior to setting the napkin outside.

Host: All chametz (leaven) that may remain, and that I am unaware of, is hereby annulled.

Interpreter: God has commanded each of us to know the condition of our own hearts. As we now enter into the worshipful celebration of the great works our God has done, let us purpose in our hearts to remove the sin that hinders us. Let us now turn our attention to the wonderful God; who is the Redeemer of Israel, the God of Abraham, Isaac, and Jacob; who is the Lord of creation, and the Savior of all who will turn to Him. Through Y'shua (Jesus), we all may approach the throne of grace boldly.

הדלקת הגרות LIGHTING THE FESTIVAL LIGHTS

Historian: As the sun is now setting, we now join God's people, Israel, throughout this world in lighting the festival lights and beginning this celebration as it has been initiated for thousands of years. We join with the great cloud of witnesses who have gone before us to the throne of God and declare that He (Who is, and Who was, and Who is to come) is worthy to be praised, honored, and glorified.

Interpreter: Tonight we stand under the banner of Israel, in the name of Y'shua, and join our hearts with God's people throughout this land, to declare that our God reigns! Our God is able to deliver! Our God saves! Our God remembers His covenant. Our God remembers His people, Israel, forever.

The Hostess lights the festival candle with her head covered. She then places her hands over her eyes and recites:

Hostess: בָּרוּךְ אַתָה יי אֱלֹהֵנוּ מֶלֶךְ הָעוֹלָם אֲשֶׁר קִדְּשָׁנוּ בְּישוּעַ הַמָשִיחַ אוֹר הָעוֹלָם וְהַפֶּסַח שֶׁלָנוּ

Ba-ruch a-tah adonai el-o-hay-nu mel-ek ha-o-lam a-sher qeed-sha-nue bee-shua ha-ma-shee-ack or ha-o-lam vi-ha-pe-sach she-la-nue.

Blessed are You, O Lord our God, King of the Universe, Who sanctifies us in Y'shua the Messiah, the light of the world and our Passover.

Part One

Kaddesh

SANCTIFYING
THE FESTIVAL

קַדֵּשׁ THE CUP OF SANCTIFICATION
Kaddesh

Have each person pour some drink into their wine glass and prepare for enjoying the first cup together.

Historian: Four cups of wine mark distinct portions of the Pesach (Passover) celebration. The four cups include: Sanctification, Deliverance, Redemption, and Praise. Together they tell the story of Israel's exodus from Egypt and mark, for all time, God's distinctive pattern for saving His people from bondage and oppression. God's use of this pattern is still used in our own lives today! The cup of sanctification, specifically, tells the story of God removing the idols of Egypt from the heart of Israel. This cup remembers the ten plagues of the past and the plagues we face yet today.

Interpreter: The first cup that we will take together is the cup of sanctification. It is during this time that we will remember the ugliness of sin. We will remember the terror of slavery and the repulsion of bondage. Sanctification places evil in its proper perspective. Evil is to be loathed, never entertained. At the same time, we remember the greatness and majesty of our God. He has sanctified us (set us apart) by the blood of Y'shua. He continues to cleanse us from all unrighteousness. He is a great God. His ways are good. His judgments are true. His mercies are everlasting!

Everyone now raise the Cup of Sanctification

קַדֵּשׁ THE CUP OF SANCTIFICATION

Host:

בָּרוּךְ אַתָּה יי אֱלֹהֵנוּ מֶלֶךְ הָעוֹלָם בּוֹרֵא פְּרִי הַגָּפֶן

Ba-ruch a-tah a-do-nai el-o-hay-nu me-lek ha-o-lam bo-ray pe-ree ha-ga-phen.

Everyone:
Blessed are You, O Lord our God, King of the Universe, Who creates the fruit of the vine.

Adult 1:
"O taste and see that the LORD is good! Blessed is the man that trusts in Him!"

Adult 2:
"This poor man cried and the LORD heard him, and saved him out of all his troubles. The angel of the LORD encamps round about them that fear Him, and delivers them!"

Adult 1:
"Such as sit in darkness and in the shadow of death, being bound in affliction and iron; because they rebelled against the words of God, and condemned the counsel of the Most High. Therefore He brought down their heart with labour; they fell down, and there was none to help. Then they cried unto the LORD in their trouble, and He saved them out of their distresses. He brought them out of darkness and the shadow of death, and broke their bands in sunder. Oh, that men would praise the LORD for His goodness, and for His wonderful works to the children of men!"

Adult 2:
"For God so loved the world, that He gave His only begotten Son, that whosoever believes in Him should not perish, but have everlasting life. For God sent not His Son into the world to condemn the world; but that the world through Him might be saved.

קִדּוּשׁ THE CUP OF SANCTIFICATION

Historian: Like Israel of old, we acknowledge our desperation in this hour. We acknowledge our need for You to deliver us from evil. We acknowledge our need for Your grace to sustain us. Blessed are You, Lord our God, the God of Abraham, Israel, and Jacob.

Interpreter: We bless You, oh Lord our God. You are able to destroy or build up, plant or uproot. You are sovereign and in control. Turn our hearts to You as we bless You in this place. Be exalted, oh God, as we join with Israel on this special evening. Tonight we pray for the peace of Jerusalem. Tonight, as we respectfully join with Israel, we pray Your blessing upon him. We pray for Your church. We pray that You will bless her with Your grace that the wonder of Your majesty may be made evident to all. Tonight, in the name of Y'shua, Your Son and our King, we submit ourselves before You as we remember Your greatness.

Host: Blessed are You, Lord our God, King of the universe, who sanctifies Israel and the festivals. You have chosen Israel and set him apart from all nations, and gave to him the holy festivals as a heritage for rejoicing and celebration. Blessed are You, Lord our God, King of the universe, who has given us life, and has sustained us, and has permitted us to reach this season.

Leaning on the left side (a reclining position), All drink the first cup together.

Song of your choice (see Section Two, page 61)

כרפם Eating the Green Vegetable
Karpas

Everyone takes a piece of green (most often parsley) from the Seder Plate.

Historian: The green vegetable is a reminder of the hyssop that was used to apply the Pascal lamb's blood to the doorpost. The salt water is a reminder of the tears shed in bondage.

Interpreter: Biblically, hyssop is a purging agent. Hyssop brought cleansing. Tonight, we recognize that coming under the protection of the Lamb's blood involves the cleansing of our hearts and lives. We acknowledge that cleansing involves tears. We identify with the suffering of Israel as slaves, and relate to the tears that living an oppressed life will bring.

Everyone: בָּרוּךְ אַתָּה יי אֱלֹהֵנוּ מֶלֶךְ הָעוֹלָם בּוֹרֵא פְּרִי הָאֲדָמָה

Ba-ruch a-tah adonai el-o-hay-nu me-lech ha-olam bo-ray pe-ree ha-a-da-ma.

Blessed are You, O Lord our God, King of the Universe, Who creates the fruit of the soil.

Everyone eats the green.

יַחַץ HIDING THE AFIKOMEN
Yachatz

The Host holds up the Afikomen Bag

Historian: The traditions regarding the hiding of the
                 Afikomen at the time of Y'shua, should be of
                 special interest to Christians today. The
                 Afikomen bag, as you see it here tonight, was
                 taken outside by the head of the house and
                 buried out of the sight of the children. Later, we
                 will see how it was found.

The Host holds up the Matzah Tosh

Interpreter: Notice that the Matzah Tosh has three compart-
                   ments, each with a piece of matzah within.
                   Rabbis over the centuries have given multiple
                   explanations for this. Yet we will not have to
                   stretch our interpretation too far to see the
                   Matzah Tosh as being a representation of the
                   unity (אֶחָד echad) of God as Father, Son, and
                   Holy Spirit. Our Host, tonight, will take the mid-
                   dle matzah, break it into two pieces, return one
                   half back to the Matzah Tosh, and place the
                   other half into the Afikomen bag. Later tonight,
                   the children will be given the opportunity to find
                   the hidden bread, and we will eat that bread as
                   our dessert.

Host: *Take the middle matzah from the Matzah Tosh,
            break it into two pieces, place one half back into
            the Matzah Tosh, and one half into the Afikomen
            bag.*

וחמץ HIDING THE AFIKOMEN

Have the children cover their eyes and hide the Afikomen bag somewhere to be found after the meal. (The finding of the Afikomen can be an energetically freeing time for the children. So, when hiding the Afikomen, beware not to put it in areas of the house where things may be broken.)

Part Two

מַגִּיד
Maggid

Reciting the Story
of Deliverance

מג'ד THE INVITATION
Maggid

Host:

Uncover the Matzah in the Matzah Tosh, pick up the Seder Plate and say:

הָא לַחְמָא עַנְיָא דִי אֲכָלוּ אַבְהָתַנָא בְּאַרְעָא דְמִצְרָיִם כָּל
דִּכְפִין יֵיתֵי וְיֵיכָל כָּל דִּצְרִיךְ יֵיתֵי וְיִפְסַח הָשַׁתָּא הָכָא
לַשָׁנָה הַבָּאָה בְּאַרְעָא דְיִשְׂרָאֵל הָשַׁתָּא עַבְדֵי לַשָׁנָה
הַבָּאָה בְּנֵי חוֹרִין

Ha lach-ma an-ya dee a-cha-lu ava-ha-ta-na be-ar-ah de-mitz-ra-yim kol dich-fin yay-tay ve-yay-chul kol ditz-rich yay-tay ve-yif-sach ha-sha-ta ha-cha la-sha-nah ha-ba-ah be-ar-ah de-yis-ra-ayl ha-sha-ta av-day la-sha-nah ha-ba-ah be-nay chorin.

This is the bread of affliction, which our ancestors ate in the land of Egypt. Let all who are hungry, come and eat. Let all who are needy, come and observe the Passover. This year we are here; next year may we be in the land of Israel. This year we are slaves; next year may we be free.

Put the Seder Plate down and cover the Matzah

Adult One: Y'shua said, "With fervent desire I have desired to eat this passover with you before I suffer."

Adult Two: "Behold, I stand at the door, and knock. If any man hear My voice, and open the door, I will come in to him, and will sup with him, and he with Me."

מ‍גּ‍י‍ד   THE INVITATION

Interpreter: Tonight, our Messiah, we accept Your invitation. Tonight we sit at Your table to enjoy Your bounty. We bless You, God our Father, our Provider. We bless You, our Hope. We bless You, our God, the One who has invited us to partake of Your goodness.

Everyone fill their wine glasses for the Second Cup

SONG of your choice (see Section Two, page 61)

מַגִּיד THE FOUR QUESTIONS

Historian:
Exodus 12:26-27 "And it shall come to pass, when your children shall say unto you, What mean ye by this service? That ye shall say, 'It is the sacrifice of the LORD's passover, who passed over the houses of the children of Israel in Egypt, when He smote the Egyptians, and delivered our houses.' And the people bowed their heads and worshiped."

Raising a child in the ways and knowledge of God has been an imperative from the beginning. It is important to God that our children understand where they came from and why they are to live the life that He has ordained. In that same way, the people of God should never forget the saving, merciful hand of God. In addition, we should never turn our backs on the Jewish culture and people who paid the price for the freedom we now enjoy.

Traditionally, the following four questions are asked by one of the youngest children present. The four questions set the stage for the recounting of the exodus story that follows.

Host:
מַה נִּשְׁתַּנָּה הַלַּיְלָה הַזֶּה מִכָּל הַלֵּילוֹת
שֶׁבְּכָל הַלֵּילוֹת אָנוּ אוֹכְלִין חָמֵץ וּמַצָּה
הַלַּיְלָה הַזֶּה כֻּלּוֹ מַצָּה
שֶׁבְּכָל הַלֵּילוֹת אָנוּ אוֹכְלִין שְׁאָר יְרָקוֹת
הַלַּיְלָה הַזֶּה מָרוֹר
שֶׁבְּכָל הַלֵּילוֹת אֵין אָנוּ מַטְבִּילִין אֲפִילוּ פַּעַם אֶחָת
הַלַּיְלָה הַזֶּה שְׁתֵּי פְעָמִים
שֶׁבְּכָל הַלֵּילוֹת אָנוּ אוֹכְלִין בֵּין יוֹשְׁבִין וּבֵין מְסֻבִּין
הַלַּיְלָה הַזֶּה כֻּלָּנוּ מְסֻבִּין

מגיד THE FOUR QUESTIONS

Ma nish-ta-nah ha-lai-lah ha-zeh mee-kol ha-lay-lot?
She-be-chol ha-lay-lot a-nu och-leen cha-maytz u-ma-tzah ha-lai-la ha-zeh ku-lo ma-tzah?
She-be-chol ha-lay-lot a-nu och-leen she-ar ye-ra-kot ha-lai-la ha-zeh ma-ror?
She-be-chol ha-lay-lot ayn a-un mat-bee-leen a-fee-lu pa-am e-chat ha-lai-la ha-zeh she-tay fe-a-meem?
She-be-chol ha-lay-lot a-nu och-leen bayn yo-she-veen u-vayn me-su-been ha-lai-la ha-zeh ku-la-nu me-su-been?

Child One: Why is this night different from all other nights? On all other nights we eat either leavened or unleavened bread; on this night why do we eat only unleavened bread?

Child Two: On all other nights we eat all kinds of vegetables; on this night why do we eat bitter herbs?

Child One: On all other nights we do not dip our vegetables even once; on this night why do we dip them twice?

Child Two: On all other nights we eat sitting upright or reclining; on this night why do we eat reclining?

The Answer - The Story of the Exodus from Egypt (portions from Deuteronomy 28:5-8)

Uncover the Matzah and begin the reply

מַגִּיד THE ANSWER

Adult One: We were once slaves of Pharaoh, in Egypt, but the Lord our God brought us out from there with a mighty hand and an outstretched arm. If God had not brought our ancestors out of Egypt, then we, our children, and grandchildren would still be Pharaoh's slaves in Egypt. Therefore, even if we all were wise and intelligent, even if we all were elders, knowledgeable in the Torah, it would still be our duty to tell the story of the exodus from Egypt. And the more one tells of the exodus from Egypt, the more that person is worthy of praise.

Adult Two: A wandering Arameean was my ancestor; he went down into Egypt and lived there as an alien, few in number, and there became a great nation, mighty and populous.

Historian: Our ancestor, Jacob, went down to Egypt in a time of famine with only the seventy members of his household. But the blessing of Abraham was upon them and they multiplied in Egypt, and became a vast throng.

Adult Two: The Egyptians treated us harshly and afflicted us, by imposing hard labor on us.

Interpreter: They enslaved us and embittered our lives, and sought to slay our children. In the same way, our lives were enslaved and embittered by the power of sin, and we suffered under the tyranny of the Prince of this world.

Adult Two: Then we cried to the Lord, the God of our ancestors; the Lord heard our voice and saw our affliction, our toil, and our oppression.

מַגִּיד THE ANSWER

Historian: The God of Abraham, Isaac, and Jacob did not forget us in our desperate plight in Egypt, but remembered His promise and had compassion on us.

Interpreter: In the same way, also, He did not forget us as we labored under the power of sin, but in compassion determined to redeem us.

Adult Two: The Lord brought us out of Egypt with a mighty hand and an outstretched arm, with a terrifying display of power, and with signs and wonders.

Historian: He worked tremendous plagues in Egypt by the hand of Moses, slaying the first-born of the Egyptians and humbling Pharaoh and his armies at the Red Sea.

Interpreter: In the same way, also, He performed signs and wonders through Y'shua, His Anointed One, giving Him up as an atoning sacrifice for the sins of the world, and raising Him from the dead, triumphing mightily over His enemies.

Adult Two: And He brought us into this place, and gave us this land, a land flowing with milk and honey.

Historian: He brought our ancestors through the wilderness, and fulfilled His promise to Abraham by giving them the land of Canaan as an inheritance.

Interpreter: In the same way, also, He has brought us into the new life of the kingdom of Heaven, and has given us the hope of the world to come.

מַגִּיד THE TEN PLAGUES

Historian: The Ten Plagues portion of the Seder turns our attention to the suffering encountered by the Egyptians due to the plagues unleashed on them.

Interpreter: Today, we recognize that living apart from God comes at a price. The wages of sin are death. Evil will exact a cost from anyone under its control. Eventually, God's judgment will fall on those who reject Him. Tonight, our hearts turn towards the suffering brought by the Ten Plagues of old, as well as the suffering of those around us in our world.

Historian: As our Host leads, let us name the plagues of old together. As we name each plague, take a drop of liquid from your wine glass with your finger, and place the liquid on a piece of matzah on your plate.

Host: דָם צְפַרְדֵּעַ כִּנִּים עָרוֹב דֶּבֶר שְׁחִין בָּרַד אַרְבֶּה
חוֹשֶׁךְ מַכַּת בְּכוֹרוֹת

Everyone: Dam [blood], Tze-far-day-ah [frogs], Kee-neem [vermin], A-rov [flies], De-ver [cattle disease], She-cheen [boils], Ba-rad [hail], Ar-beh [locust], Cho-shech [darkness], Ma-kat Be-cho-rot [death of the first-born]
Additional (optional): the Holocaust, cancer, A.I.D.S, etc.

Host: God our Father, merciful God, we acknowledge Your saving grace. We praise You for Your wonderful works towards us. We acknowledge that

מגיד THE TEN PLAGUES

Host:　　You are a Holy God. Tonight we ask for Your compassion to pour out upon our world. Bless your people Israel. Bless Your church. Bring justice to those who are oppressed, healing to those who are sick, righteousness to those who wander without You, and peace to those who are not complete in You.

Interpreter:　　Yes Father, may peace reign in Jerusalem in our day. May our mighty King set up His throne in the city of David. Tonight we join our hearts with the Apostles of old as they cried out, "Come Quickly Lord Jesus!"

דַּיֵּנוּ DAI-YEY-NU

Historian: God was under no obligation to save Israel out of his distress. Yet, He was gracious and merciful. Dai-yey-nu ('it would have been enough') attempts to show the magnitude of Gods favor towards Israel.

Interpreter: Today, we too can join with Israel in an overwhelming recognition that God has abundantly and incredibly done much more for us than we will ever deserve. With a grateful heart for all He has accomplished, we say, "It would have been enough."

Adult One: How numerous are the favors God has bestowed on us!

Host: Had He brought us out of Egypt, and not punished the Egyptians.

Everyone: Dai-yey-nu

Host: Had He punished the Egyptians, and not slain their first-born.

Everyone: Dai-yey-nu

Host: Had He put to death their first-born, and not divided the Red Sea for us.

Everyone: Dai-yey-nu

Host: Had He divided the Red Sea for us, and not fed us manna.

דַּיֵּנוּ DAI-YEY-NU

Everyone: Dai-yey-nu

Host: Had He fed us manna, and not given us the Sabbath.

Everyone: Dai-yey-nu

Host: Had He given us the Sabbath, and not brought us to Mt. Sinai.

Everyone: Dai-yey-nu

Host: Had He brought us to Mt. Sinai, and not given us the Torah.

Everyone: Dai-yey-nu

Host: Had He given us the Torah, and not brought us to the land of Israel.

Everyone: Dai-yey-nu

Host: Had He brought us to Israel, and not given us the Temple.

Everyone: Dai-yey-nu

Host: Had He given us the Temple, and not sent us the Messiah.

Everyone: Dai-yey-nu

Host: Had He sent us the Messiah, and not given Him up to die for our sins.

רַּיֵּינוּ DAI-YEY-NU

Everyone: Dai-yey-nu

Host: Had He given Him up to die for our sins, and not raised Him up to His right hand in heaven.

Everyone: Dai-yey-nu

Host: Had He raised Him up to His right hand, and not promised that He would return in Glory!

Everyone: Dai-yey-nu

Historian: How much more, then, should we be grateful to God for the many favors He has bestowed on us: He brought us out of Egypt, punished the Egyptians, put to death their first-born, divided the Red Sea for us, fed us with manna, gave us the Sabbath, brought us to Mt. Sinai, gave us the Torah, brought us to the land of Israel, gave us the Temple, sent us the Messiah, gave Him up to die for our sins, raised Him to His right hand in heaven, and promised that He would return in glory!

Interpreter: Yes, Dai-yey-nu. Yet there is more. Each one of us who have the testimony of Y'shua in our hearts can add to this list many personal accounts of God intervening and changing our lives forever.

Adult One: For Your mercies, which are new every morning, we give You thanks.

דַּיֵּנוּ DAI-YEY-NU

Adult Two: For Your love, which knows no bounds, we give You thanks.

Adult One: For making us accepted in the Beloved, we give You thanks.

Adult Two: For giving us the seal of Your Holy Spirit, we give You thanks.

Adult One: For writing our names in the Lambs book of Life, we give You thanks.

Everyone: Dai-yey-nu

SONG Dayenu (found on page 62)

פסח The Essentials of the
Passover **Passover Seder**

Historian: Rabbi Gamaliel taught:"Whoever does not
explain the following three elements of the
Passover Seder has not fulfilled his duty—the
Passover Lamb, the Unleavened Bread, and the
Bitter Herbs."

Host:

Hold up the Lamb Shank bone from the Seder Plate

What was the reason for the Passover offering
which our fathers ate in days of the Temple? It is
because the Holy One, blessed be He, passed
over the houses of our forefathers in Egypt as it
is written in the Bible: "And you shall say it is
the Passover offering for the Eternal God Who
passed over the houses of the children of Israel
in Egypt when He smote the Egyptians and
spared our houses. And the people bowed and
worshiped."

Interpreter: Y'shua is the Passover Lamb that was slain for
the world!

Host:

Pick up the Matzah from the Seder Plate

What is the reason for the Matzah we eat? It is
because there was not time for the dough of our
ancestors in Egypt to become leavened, before
the Ruler of all, the Holy One, redeemed them.

פּסח The Essentials of the Passover Seder

Interpreter: Y'shua was without sin (leaven). Yet He was pierced and broken for us!

Host:

Pick up the Maror from the Seder Plate

What is the reason for the bitter herbs we eat? They are eaten to recall that the Egyptians embittered the lives of our forefathers in Egypt.

Interpreter: Yes, sin brings the curse. It is a bitter curse that is hard to digest. Yet, Y'shua became a curse for us as He died on the cross.

Historian: In every generation one must look upon himself as if he personally had come out of Egypt. As the Bible says, "It is because of that which the Eternal God did to me when I went forth from Egypt." For it was not our forefathers alone whom the Holy One, blessed be He, redeemed; He redeemed us also with them, as it is said, "He brought us out from there, that He might lead us to, and give us the land that He promised to our forefathers."

Everyone:

Raise the Second Cup of wine and say:

Therefore, it is our duty to thank and to praise in song and prayer, to glorify and extol Him who performed all these wonders for our forefathers,

פסח The Essentials of the Passover Seder

Everyone: and for us. He brought us out from slavery to freedom, from anguish to joy, from sorrow to festivity, from darkness to great light. Let us, therefore, sing before Him a new song. PRAISE THE ETERNAL GOD!

Put down the Second Cup of wine

Songs from The first part of the Hallel - (Psalms 113-114)

Historian: When Israel went forth from Egypt, the house of Jacob from a people of strange tongue; Judah became His sanctuary, Israel His dominion. The sea beheld and fled, the Jordan turned back. The mountains skipped like rams, the hills like lambs. What ails thee, O sea, that thou didst flee, Jordan, that thou turnest back; you mountains, that you skip like rams, you hills, like lambs?

Adult One: Tremble, thou earth, at the presence of the Eternal God, at the presence of the God of Jacob; Who turns the rock into a pool of water, the flint into a fountain of water!

פסח The Cup of Deliverance

Adult One: Blessed are You, Eternal God, who has delivered us with an outstretched arm.

Adult Two: Blessed are You, our gracious King, who has delivered our lives from destruction and placed us within Your everlasting kingdom.

Everyone:
Lift up the Second Glass of wine and lean to the left

Host: בָּרוּךְ אַתָה יי אֱלֹהֵנוּ מֶלֶךְ הָעוֹלָם בּוֹרֵא פְּרִי הַגָּפֶן

Ba-ruch a-tah adonai el-o-hay-nu me-lek ha-o-lam bo-ray pe-ree ha-ga-phen.

Everyone: Blessed are You, O Lord our God, King of the Universe, Who creates the fruit of the vine.

Everyone drink the cup

EATING THE ELEMENTS FROM THE SEDER PLATE (THE MEAL)

רָחְצָה

Rachtzah

Washing the Hands

Historian: Before any food may be eaten, the hands must be washed.

Interpreter: Just as Y'shua began His final Passover Seder by washing His disciple's feet, so we, too, will wash prior to eating the Passover elements.

Everyone: *Using the water in front of you, everyone wash your hands and say the following blessing:*

Blessed are You, Lord our God, ruler of the universe, Who made us holy with His commandments, and commanded us concerning the washing of hands.

מוֹצִיא

Motzi

The Matzah

Interpreter: It is now time to share together the elements from the Seder Plate beginning with the Matzah (the unleavened bread).

Host:
Pick up the Matzah from off the Seder Plate

בָּרוּךְ אַתָה יי אֱלֹהֵנוּ מֶלֶךְ הָעוֹלָם הַמּוֹצִיא לֶחֶם מִן הָאָרֶץ

Ba-ruch a-tah adonai elo-hay-nu me-lech ha-o-lam ha-mo-tzee le-chem min ha-a-retz.

Everyone: Blessed are You, O Lord our God, King of the Universe, Who brings forth bread from the earth.

EATING THE ELEMENTS FROM THE SEDER PLATE (THE MEAL)

Host: בָּרוּךְ אַתָּה יי אֱלֹהֵנוּ מֶלֶךְ הָעוֹלָם אֲשֶׁר קִדְּשָׁנוּ בְּמִצְוֹתָיו
וְצִוָּנוּ עַל אֲכִילַת מַצָּה

Ba-rch a-tah adonai elo-hay-nu me-lech ha-o-la
a-sher kid-de-sha-nu be-mitz-vo-tav ve-tzi-va-nu
al a-chi-lat matzah.

Everyone: Blessed are You, O Lord our God, King of the
Universe, Who has sanctified us with Your commandments and commanded us concerning the
eating of unleavened bread.

Everyone eat a small piece of Matzah from the Seder Plate

מָרוֹר

Maror

The
Maror

Interpreter: Now it is time to mix a piece of
Matzah with the Maror (bitter herbs). We do this
to be reminded of the bitterness of slavery and
oppression. As a special note, this was most like-
ly the time during Y'shua's final Passover meal
(the Lord's supper) where He handed the
Matzah/Maror combination to Judas Iscariot
who then left to betray Y'shua.

Everyone:

*Take a small piece of Matzah from the Seder Plate and spread
some Maror on it*

Host:: בָּרוּךְ אַתָּה יי אֱלֹהֵנוּ מֶלֶךְ הָעוֹלָם אֲשֶׁר קִדְּשָׁנוּ בְּמִצְוֹתָיו וְצִוָּנוּ
עַל אֲכִילַת מָרוֹר

Everyone: Ba-ruch a-tah adonai elo-hay-nu me-lech
ha-o-lam a-sher kid-de-sha-nu be-mitz-vo-tav
ve-tzi-va-nu al a-chi-lat maror.

Blessed are You, O Lord our God, King of the

מָרוֹר
The
Maror

Universe, Who has sanctified us with Your commandments and commanded us concerning the eating of bitter herbs.

Everyone eat the Matzah/Maror combination

כּוֹרֵך
Korech
The
Korech

The Charoseth

Interpreter: While the maror reminds us of the bitterness of slavery, the Charoseth reminds us of the sweetness of freedom. Tonight we are free in Y'shua. Now, because of Y'shua, no enemy that attempts to conquer will be victorious, and no weapon formed against us will stand.

Everyone:
Spread some Charoseth on a piece of Matzah and eat it together

The Egg

Historian: The egg we now eat reminds us of the destruction of the Temple, shortly after the return to heaven of our Lord. Since the time of the Temple's destruction, the Jewish community has been in mourning. Tonight, we join them as we look forward to a day where a new Temple will be placed in Jerusalem, and a Son of David will once again judge between the pillars.

Everyone:
Dip the Egg into the salt water and eat together

שֻׁלְחָן
עוֹרֵך
SHULCHAN
ORECH
The
Festival
Meal

Host: The festive meal is now presented. Enjoy!

Take however long necessary to enjoy the food that has been prepared, and the people that you are with. Give the children an opportunity to stretch and burn off some energy.

Once the meal is complete, gather everyone back to the table with a couple of songs.

SONG of your choice (Section Two, page 61)

Part Three

בָּרֵךְ

Barech

Grace after the Meal

בּרך FINDING THE AFIKOMEN

Everyone pour the Third Cup of wine

Historian: The Afikomen (which means dessert) is our dessert. Earlier we learned of the Afikomen being buried outside the house. Tonight, our host has hidden the Afikomen within the home. Now, it is time for the children to find it. Traditionally, the child who has successfully retrieved the Afikomen would bring it back to the father, and then begin to negotiate for a grand prize. The father would take the Afikomen from the child, after they had agreed on a price, and then give the child a token that promised to give full payment at a later date. This promise was called "the promise of the father."

Interpreter: The Apostle Paul told the Greeks in Athens that, at the time of Noah, God purposely hid Himself from mankind. Yet there is a place within each person that continues to search for God. Finding God has been made simple by Y'shua. He is the Bread of Life that was broken and buried for us to find. Those who find Him are then brought into a new relationship with the Father, who gives to us His promise. Y'shua, Himself, identifies the promise of the Father as the Holy Spirit. Today, everyone who finds the Lord receives "the Promise of the Father" (the Holy Spirit). Everyone who has "the Promise of the Father" is guaranteed that this gift is merely a down payment of what is to come.

Let the children go to find the Afikomen

בְּרֵךְ FINDING THE AFIKOMAN

Once found, the host should reward the child, take the Afikomen, and distribute it to all.

Adult One: "I am the vine and you are the branches: he that abides in Me, and I in him, the same brings forth much fruit: for without Me you can do nothing."

Interpreter: The Afikomen (Y'shua) is our dessert. No one is ever forced to eat a dessert. In fact, a dessert is something to be enjoyed and savored. It was at this point, during the Lord's Last Passover, that He said, "This is My body which is given for you; do this in remembrance of Me." Now is our time to come into the presence of our Messiah, as we take Him into ourselves.

Host: Lets now eat the Afikomen together.

All eat the Afikomen

Host: Let us say grace.

Everyone: May the name of the Holy One be blessed from now and for evermore.

Host: With the permission of all present, let us praise our God, Whose food we have eaten.

Everyone: Blessed be our God, Whose food we have eaten and in Whose goodness we live. Blessed be He, and blessed be His name.

Adult One: Blessed are You, King of the Universe, Who sustains the worlds in His goodness, with grace, loving kindness, and mercy. He gives food to all.

בְּרֵךְ FINDING THE AFIKOMEN

Adult Two: Blessed are You, King of the Universe, Who pro vides all and sustains all.

Host: For all Your blessings, our God, we thank You and bless You. May Your name be blessed in the mouth of all the living, at all times, and for all time! Eternal God, have mercy on Israel, Your people; on Jerusalem, Your city; and Zion, the dwelling place of Your glory; and on the royal house of David, Your anointed; and on the great and holy Temple called by Your name. Our God, our Father, be our Shepherd.

Interpreter: Y'shua, we come to You. Be in us as we are in You. By Your Spirit, walk with us and talk with us, as You did years ago with Adam in the Garden of Eden. Be our help and our stability as we purpose to live our lives under Your authori ty and in Your presence.

בְּרֵךְ THE CUP OF REDEMPTION

Historian: The hosts of Pharaoh followed Israel to the shores of the Red Sea. With nowhere to turn, Israel waited for their redemption. When the sea opened up, Israel walked across to a new life. When the sea closed, a permanent ownership change took place. Pharaoh would no longer have any influence in the lives of the Israelites.

Interpreter: With sanctification and deliverance behind us, after having eaten of the Lord's goodness, we turn our attention to redemption. The Cup of

Redemption has special meaning to the body of Y'shua. It was at this point in the Lord's last Passover that He said, "This is My blood." It is the Blood of Y'shua that gives us our identity, citizenship, and authority. It is the Blood of Y'shua that transfers our ownership from the kingdom of darkness to the kingdom of light.

Everyone raise the Third Cup

Host: בָּרוּךְ אַתָּה יי אֱלֹהֵנוּ מֶלֶךְ הָעוֹלָם בּוֹרֵא פְּרִי הַגָּפֶן

Ba-ruch a-tah adonai el-o-hay-nu me-lek ha-o-lam bo-ray pe-ree ha-ga-phen.

Everyone: Blessed are You, O Lord our God, King of the Universe, Who creates the fruit of the vine.

Leaning on the left side, all drink the Third Cup

Adult One: We have been bought with a price. You, Lord our God, have redeemed our lives from destruction.

Adult Two: We are now a people who before were not a people. We are now a chosen generation, a royal priesthood, a holy nation, a peculiar people; that we may show forth the praises of Him who has called us out of darkness into His marvelous light.

Historian: Y'shua said, "Those who believe in Me will never thirst!"

Everyone: Today, O God, we have a place in Your kingdom because of the redeeming blood of Y'shua. We believe Your Word! We hold Your word above all that we see and hear. We acknowledge

Your right of ownership in our lives. We acknowledge You as our sovereign God. We declare that You are the only one who can satisfy our soul.

בְּרַךְ ELIJAH'S PLACE

Historian: A special place has been set at the table anticipating and hoping for the arrival of the Elijah, the prophet. Elijah was prophesied to return and announce the arrival of the Messiah. Traditionally, at this point in the evening, a child was sent to open the door and invite Elijah into the home.

Interpreter: While speaking with His disciples, Y'shua told them that Elijah had already come. His name was John the Baptist. Tonight we will fill a glass of wine for Elijah and join the Jewish community in singing a song that calls for Elijah to come. This evening, however, our hearts are fixed into the future when the Jewish Messiah will return and, this time, claim His rightful place as the King of kings and the Lord of lords here on earth.

Have a child go and open the front door

SONG Ay-lee-ya-hu Ha-na-vee (found on page 63)

Host: Elijah the prophet, Elijah the Tishbite, Elijah the Gileadite, may he come speedily in our days with Messiah the Son of David!

If Elijah and the Messiah have not returned have the child close the door

Part Four

הלל

Hallel

Praise

הלל THE REMAINING HALLEL PSALMS 115 - 118

Historian: Those who have been sanctified, delivered, fed, and redeemed cannot contain the praise of the Most High God. Praise must flow from God's people or the rocks will cry out. When Israel found himself free on the banks of the Red Sea, the instruments sounded, the tambourine played, the ladies danced, and the entire nation sang the song of Moses.

Interpreter: For us today, all songs of praise are a mere dress rehearsal for that glorious day when the song of Moses will erupt in heaven. A pure song of praise will fill the air, as all of God's people will sound the greatness of our King!

Host: Not unto us, O Lord, not unto us, but to Your name give glory, because of Your mercy, because of Your truth!

Adult One: O Israel, trust in the Lord; He is their help and their shield!

Adult Two: O house of Aaron, trust in the Lord; He is their help and shield!

Everyone: You who fear the Lord, trust in the Lord; He is their help and shield!

Interpreter: He will bless those who fear the Lord, both small and great!

Historian: The heaven, even the heaven of heavens, are the Lord's but the earth He has given to the children of men.

Everyone:	We will bless the Lord from this time forth and forevermore!
Adult One:	Gracious is the Lord, and righteous; Yes, our God is merciful!
Everyone:	I will walk before the Lord in the land of the living! I will take up the cup of salvation, and call upon the name of the Lord! I will pay my vows in the presence of all His people!
Historian:	Praise the Lord, all you Gentiles! Laud Him all you peoples!
Everyone:	For His merciful kindness is great towards us, and the truth of the Lord endures forever!
Host:	Praise the Lord! O give thanks to the Lord, for He is good!
Everyone:	For His mercy endures forever!
Host:	Let Israel now say!
Everyone:	His mercy endures forever!
Host:	Let the house of Aaron now say!
Everyone:	His mercy endures forever!
Host:	Let those who fear the Lord now say!
Everyone:	His mercy endures forever!
Adult One:	I called on the Lord in my distress; the Lord answered me and set me in a broad place!
Adult Two:	The Lord is on my side; I will not fear! What can man do to me?

Historian: It is better to trust in the Lord than to put confidence in man. It is better to trust in the Lord than to put confidence in princes.

Interpreter: The Lord is my strength and my song, and He has become my salvation!

Historian: Shouts of joy and victory resound in the tents of the righteous of the Lord!

Everyone: Open to me the gates of righteousness; I will go through them, and I will praise the Lord!

Host: I will praise You, for You have answered me, and have become my salvation!

Everyone: The stone, which the builders rejected, has become the chief cornerstone!

Host: This is marvelous in our eyes!

Everyone: This is the day the Lord has made; we will rejoice and be glad in it!

Adult One: Save now, I pray, O Lord; O Lord, I pray, send now prosperity!

Everyone: Blessed is He who comes in the name of the Lord!

Adult Two: We have blessed You from the house of the Lord!

Everyone: God is the Lord, and He has given us light; bind the sacrifice with cords to the horns of the altar.

Historian:	You are my God, and I will praise You!
Everyone:	You are my God, I will exalt You!
Host:	O Give thanks to the Lord, for He is good!
Everyone:	For His mercy endures forever!

הלל THE CUP OF PRAISE

Historian:	After drinking the Third Cup (the Cup of Redemption) at His final Passover Seder, Y'shua made an interesting statement, "Verily I say unto you, I will drink no more of the fruit of the vine, until that day that I drink it new in the kingdom of God." The Cup of Praise is being reserved for a time in the future, when all of God's people can sing a pure song of praise. And all evil on earth is dealt a final blow: death itself being defeated. Today, all praise is a mere warm-up for that day. As we now fill our glasses one more time, we turn our attention to that time when all things will once more be subject to God.
Interpreter:	As we lift our glasses, we turn our attention to the day when a voice in heaven will cry out, "Praise the Lord, all you servants of the Lord, all you who fear Him both small and great!" Our response on that day will be...
Everyone:	Alleluia! For the Lord God Omnipotent reigns!

Fill your wine glasses and raise them

הלל The Cup of Praise

Host:

בָּרוּךְ אַתָּה יי אֱלֹהֵנוּ מֶלֶךְ הָעוֹלָם בּוֹרֵא פְּרִי הַגָּפֶן

Ba-ruch a-tah adonai el-o-hay-nu me-lek
ha-o-lam bo-ray pe-ree ha-ga-phen.

Everyone: Blessed are You, O Lord our God, King of the
Universe, Who creates the fruit of the vine.

Leaning on the left side, all drink the Forth Cup

הלל Closing

Host:

חֲסַל סִדּוּר פֶּסַח כְּהִלְכָתוֹ כְּכָל מִשְׁפָּטוֹ וְחֻקָּתוֹ כַּאֲשֶׁר
זָכִינוּ לְסַדֵּר אוֹתוֹ זַךְ שׁוֹכֵן מְעוֹנָה
קוֹמֵם קְהַל עֲדַת מִי מָנָה בְּקָרוֹב נַהֵל נִטְעֵי כַנָּה פְּדוּיִם
לְצִיּוֹן בְּרִנָּה

Cha-sal see-dur pe-sach ke-heel-cha-to ke-chol
meesh-pa-to ve-chu-ka-to ka-a-sher za-chee-nu
le-sa-der o-to zach sho-chayn me-o-nah ko-
maym ke-hal a-dat meema-nah be-ka-rov na-
hayl neet-ay cha-nah pe-du-yeem le-tzee-yon be-
ree-nah

The Passover Seder is now ended, according to
all custom, statute, and law. As we were worthy
to celebrate it this year, so may we perform it in
the future. O Pure One in heaven, restore the
congregation of Israel in Your love. Speedily
lead Your redeemed people to Zion in joy.

לְשָׁנָה הַבָּאָה בִּירוּשָׁלָיִם

Le-sha-nah ha-ba-ah bee-ru-sha-la-yim

Next Year in Jerusalem!

Everyone:	Le-sha-nah ha-ba-ah, Le-sha-nah ha-ba-ah, Le-sha-nah ha-ba-ah bee-ru-sha-la-yim
Host:	Glorious is He, May He build His Temple speedily in our days. O God, build Your Temple soon!
Interpreter:	Yes, come quickly Lord Jesus, come quickly and in our day! O God our Father, rebuild the temple in Jerusalem, and set Your Son to judge between the pillars. Bring Your peace to Jerusalem, that all may know that You are God and God alone. Come quickly Lord Jesus, that all things may be set to right, and righteousness may rule in the land of the living.

Song Adir-Hu (found on page 64)

The Seder Is Now Concluded

The Seder is now complete. You may dismiss at this point or continue to worship in song.

Section Two

Passover Songs

Organized and Arranged
by Mr. Eric Renzema

The following pages include three traditional Passover songs. Have fun with these songs. They are public domain so they may be copied and distributed. MIDI files for these songs maybe found on the internet.

In addition to the traditional songs, there are spots for three other songs to fill your evening (pages 23, 29 and 46). Fill these spots with songs that have meaning for you in the spirit of the Lord's death, burial, and resurrection.

Dayenu

Eliyahu Ha- Navi

Adir-Hu

Ba - chur hu,   A - dir hu,   A - dir hu   Yiv - neh ve - ito be - ka - rov   Bim - hei - r - a - h,
Ha - dur hu,   ga - dol hu,   da - gul hu
Chas - sid hu,   va - tik hu,   za - kai hu
Ka - bir hu,   ta - hor hu,   ya - chid hu
No - ra hu,   la - mud hu,   mel - ech hu
Po - deh hu,   sa - giv hu,   iiz - uz hu
Rach - um hu,   tza - dik hu,   ka - dosh hu
            shad - dai hu,   ta - kif hu

bim - hei - rah,   Beya - mei - nu be - ka' - a - rov   Ehl be - nei,   Ehl be - nei   Be - me veit - cha be -

- ka' - a - rov

Section Three

פסח

Preparing
the
Passover Meal

פֶּסַח Preparation for the Seder

(The Passover Meal)

The remainder of this book (along with the appendix) will give
practical guidelines for preparing and enjoying the Passover.
You will notice the great amount of preparation time required
for the event. Because of this fact, a family should be united in
a desire to prepare and celebrate the Passover. In addition,
Passover preparation should involve everyone in the household.
The feast was designed by God as a family event to be appreci-
ated by young and old alike. Don't exclude the children from
the Passover meal but include them from the beginning of your
preparation. The children in a household should be given every
opportunity to help prepare both the house and the meal. Build
excitement and anticipation as the evening approaches. Look
forward to a fun evening of good food, special songs, a unique
tie with our religious roots, and worship of our God through
our Messiah.

When to Celebrate Passover

There is a distinct difference between the Jewish and Christian
calendars. The Jewish religious calendar is tied to the lunar
cycle and dates are set according to the feasts. Passover is celebrated annually on the 15th of the first month (Adar). Adar is
the first month of spring and begins like all other Jewish
months, at the new moon. In contrast, the Christian Church's
celebration of Palm Sunday, Good Friday, and Easter are tied to
specific days of the week. As a result of these differences, the
Passover celebration rarely coincides with the church's celebrations.

Christians who desire to celebrate the Passover often wish to do
so while the church's attentions are focused on the days sur-
rounding Easter. Good Friday is usually a preferred date as
much of the Passover encompasses the work of the Lord on the
cross. Choosing which date to celebrate Passover becomes a

---

matter of personal choice. However, determining the Jewish date for Passover, and planning your celebration at that time is preferable. After all, we are joining Israel in their celebration, not attempting to create our own.

Once the date for the Passover celebration has been determined, we need to set a time to begin the gathering. The Jewish day begins at a different time than our normal day. We begin a new day at 12:00am. The Jewish community begins their day at sunset. Traditionally, the Passover begins at this time. Depending on where you live, this could mean that your celebration will begin as late as 8:30pm. You may wish to adjust this late start time. But keep in mind that a Seder can take as long as four hours (the meal included).

How Many People Do You Invite to the Seder?

The rabbinic limit to a Passover Seder is twenty people. This is a good maximum number to use when planning your Seder. Keeping the number of people below twenty provides for an intimate atmosphere. When the number exceeds twenty people, the evening becomes more of a teaching time than a time of worship.

If you, or your church, are more interested in hosting a Passover teaching than conducting your own Seder, there are a number of good teachings available from a variety of Messianic sources. In addition, there are a number of Messianic Jews who are available to come to your church and present a Passover overview.

Is There a Dress Code for the Passover Seder?

The evening of the Passover Seder is a special time. While there is no defined dress code, you will want everyone to dress up. Dressing up demonstrates that the evening is different and, thus, helps to provide an atmosphere of reverence.

Items Necessary for the Celebration

You will need to find the following items prior to the Passover Celebration (most items can be seen on the front cover). These items can be easily found on the Internet or in most Judaica shops:

1. Seder Plate (1 plate per 7 people)

The Seder Plate is the focal point of the evening. While any plate may be used to hold the Passover clements, many Jewish households have a special plate used solely for this purpose. The Seder Plate can become ornate and pricey. Yet you should be able to find a nice plate for under $40.00.

During the meal, the Seder plate will hold the following items:

    Lamb Shank Bone (1 per plate)
    Boiled Eggs (1 per plate)
    Charoset (1 dish per plate) (see recipes in the appendix)
    Maror (1 dish per plate) (see recipes in the appendix)
    Onions (1 per plate)
    Parsley (1 small bunch per plate)

2. Matzah Tosh (1)

The Matzah Tosh is a three-compartment bag that will hold three special pieces of unleavened bread during the Seder. These bags are available in varying degrees of detail and price.

3. Afikomen Bag or Napkin

The Afikomen bag is a small linen container that will hold a half piece of Matzah during the Seder. Some families use a napkin to wrap the Afikomen while others buy ornate bags.

4. Napkin and Feather

You will need a linen napkin and a feather to be used by the host to find and dispose of pieces of leaven left behind.

5. Items for each Place Setting at the Table

In addition to normal dinnerware, you will need to add the following to each place at the Passover table:

Small cup filled with salt water by each plate
Small cup filled with water by each plate

6. Candle for the Hostess to Light

The Seder will begin with the Hostess lighting a candle. This candle will burn during the entire evening.

7. Enough Haggadahs (copies of Section One) for everyone to be able to read and participate.

8. Extra Matzah (unleavened bread)

Matzah is available in many grocery stores. In addition to the Matzah needed for the Matzah Tosh, you will want to have a few pieces of Matzah available around the table.

9. A Place Setting for Elijah

A favorite Passover tradition is to prepare for the possible coming of Elijah to the Seder. Somewhere on your table, set up a complete place setting reserved for Elijah.

Preparation of the House

The time of Passover is often associated with spring-cleaning. In fact, many of the traditional requirements for preparing a home for Passover necessitated a thorough cleaning of the house. Preparing your home for Passover can be as involved as you wish to make it. The idea behind the preparation is to remove all leaven products. Any item that was made using yeast, of any sort, should be dealt with.

Use your imagination when preparing the room where the Seder will be enjoyed. Try to make the area special. You can use decor to create an atmosphere of celebration.

Food for the Passover Meal

Midway through the Passover liturgy, there is a break to eat a meal. The meal itself is designed to be memorable. Think in terms of a large "Thankgiving Day" style of meal. Yet this meal will involve foods that you and your family may not be accustomed to eating. Lamb, special soups, and Passover cakes make this meal unique and exciting. See the Appendix for further help in this area.

פסח

Appendix

Samples for the Seder

פסח Sample Menu

Contributed by Mrs. Joan Greenfield

Seder Plate: (Hostess)

1) **Charoset**
    - 1 large apple - Golden Delicious or Granny Smith finely chopped.
    - ¼ cup pecans (chips)
    - ¼ teaspoon cinnamon
    - ¼ cup honey
    - 2 Tablespoons sweet wine
    - Serves 10 people: double recipe if more than 10.
    - Cover. Keep refrigerated.

2) **Maror**
    - Horseradish

3) **Shank Bone**(s)

4) **Parsley**
    - ½ a bunch serves approximately 20 people.
    - Use remainder for garnishing food plates.

5) **Roasted Eggs**
    - Jumbo size
    - ½ egg per person, plus the number of whole eggs for the number of Seder plates (2-3).
    - Boil eggs
    - Shell eggs
    - Poke eggs with pin to keep eggs from exploding!
    - Grease shallow baking dish
    - Roast eggs in oven at 325 degrees for 15 minutes.
    - Keep 2-3 eggs whole for Seder plates, cut rest of the eggs in half.
    - Place eggs on egg plates, cover, and refrigerate.

6) (3) **Onions**
    - Whole, unpeeled

Soup: (Hostess)
    - Homemade soup - Make 1-2 days ahead.

Relish Tray:
    - Seedless Grapes - red or black

- Mini Carrots
- Colby/Cheddar Cheese - small cubes
- Radishes
- <u>Kosher</u> Dill Pickles - thin spears
- Black and/or Green Olives
- Green/Red Peppers - strips
- Add or delete any items to fit your taste.

Matzoh Bread: (Hostess)
- 1 box - Plain flavor - no onion or garlic.
- Lightly salted, if possible.

Meat: (Hostess)
- Leg of Lamb - A good price is $1.89 - $2.50 per pound - wait for sale - usually runs one week prior to Good Friday.
- Approximately ½ pound per person (Example: 6 pounds will serve 12 people).
- Season with spices or marinate meat for flavor.
- Roast at 325 degrees - 6 lb. approximately = 4 hours
- 10 1b. approximately = 6 hours
- Gravy - Make from meat juice.

Vegetables: (choose two)
- California Mix: broccoli, cauliflower, & carrots
- Corn
- Green-Bean Casserole
- Yams
- Mashed potatoes

Salad: (choose one)
- Jello Salad
- Ambrosa Fruit Salad

Dessert:
- Passover Cake - no leavening agent in recipe.
- Ice cream
- Hot Fudge (Hostess)
- Strawberries - fresh or frozen/mashed (Hostess)

Drinks: (Hostess)
- Ice Water - (optional: with lemon slice)
- Sweet Passover Wine
- Sparkling Grape Juice - for kids & pregnant mothers
- Tea (decaf)

Candy Cups: Optional
- Candy/Nuts - in cups

Party Favors: Optional
- Used to make the evening memorable for all.
(Passover coloring books are available for the children.)

פסח SAMPLE GUEST LIST AND FOOD ASSIGNMENT

Contributed by Mrs. Joan Greenfield

Guest List:

- Mark calendar - date and time
- 1-2 weeks prior to Passover make guest list. Invite immediate family first, than add to your list those when God lays on your heart to invite.
- Keep guest list at 20 or less.
- Call people on your list - refer to "Menu" list for food choices.
- Inform guests of time, place, dress attire, etc.
- Follow up a week before Passover with a confirmation call to your guests.

Food Assignment:

Host & Hostess (5)
- Meat: lamb & gravy
- Soup
- Drinks: tea, wine, water, lemon,(sparkling) grape juice
- Seder Plate:
    - Charoset
    - eggs
    - onions
    - horseradish
    - parsley
- (1 box) Matzoh Bread
- Dessert
    - Hot Fudge
    - Strawberries
- Miscellaneous
    - Small plastic cups
    - Dessert plates
    - Soup bowls
    - Decorative napkins

Mom & Dad (2)
- Mashed potatoes
- Yams
- Candy/nut cups
- (2) Chairs

Jake & Tonya (4)
- (4) Chairs
- Vegetable

Doug & Chris (3)
- (4) Chairs
- Vegetable
- Cake

Bob W. (1)
- Ice Cream

Kyle R. (1)
- Fruit Salad

Total: 16 Guests

פֶּסַח SAMPLE PASSOVER SCHEDULE

Contributed by Mrs. Joan Greenfield

Passover Minus 4 Days:
Call guests to confirm and give out information:
- Get exact count
- Food assignment - refer to "Guest List/Food Assignment"
- Date
- Time: Promptly at 5:30pm
- Place: Host & Hostess's home
- Emphasize: Bring food **ready to serve**.
              Dress your best - no jeans!
- Review "Menu" and make grocery list.
- Grocery shop - except for produce
- Clean house
- Start memorizing blessing - both in Hebrew and English.

Passover Minus 3 Days:
- Make name place cards for guests (optional).
- Thaw lamb (if frozen)
- Make ice cubes (1 freezer bag full)
- Bottle water (2 gallons)

Passover Minus 2 Days:
- Buy produce
- Make soup
- Make hot fudge

Passover Minus 1 Day:
- Chill sparkling grape juice & wine.
- Fill pitchers with water and chill.

Set Table
- Note: If it is a matter of expense and/or convenience, paper/plastic products may be used instead of china, glassware and stemware. Otherwise, use the best that you have.
  - White table clothes
  - Plates
  - Stemware

פֶּסַח SAMPLE PASSOVER SCHEDULE

Passover Minus 1 Day:
- Drinking glasses
- Wine glasses (demi size)
- Napkins/napkin ring holders (optional)
- Place setting for Elijah - plate & chalice
- Seder plates with shank bones, with 2 small cups per plate (for horseradish & Charoset).
- Salt/pepper (2-3 sets)
- Honey, sugar bowl & sugar spoon (for tea)
- 2-3 Small plates for broken Matzah bread.
- Haggadahs - every other place (Host & Hostess have their own).
- Song sheets - every other place
- Candles/matches

Chairs
- If there are not enough chairs for the number of guests, borrow folding chairs from the guests that will be attending.

Decorate Room
- Make the room and dining room table festive, to create a celebrative atmosphere.
- Be creative; use pictures, banners, candles, greenery, etc.

Host/Hostess Place Setting
- Head coverings for Host & Hostess.
- 4 small Passover wine cups (optional)
- "Token" for Afikomen

Food Table - If space is affordable a card table with white tablecloth. Keep platters/bowls of food on this table to keep dining table less cluttered.

Host's Table
- Card table with white tablecloth.
- Afikomen Bag (dessert)
- Matzoh Tosh Bag - 3 compartments
- Tape player & tape (pre-arranged/recorded songs)
- Large washbowl & linen napkin

Set out in kitchen
- Dessert plates

- Mugs (for tea)
- Soup bowls & soup ladle
- Ladle for strawberries
- Ladle for hot fudge
- Ice cream scoop
- Sharp cake knife/spatula
- Meat platter
- Meat fork
- Serving spoons
- Gravy bowl & ladle

Tray
- Count out small plastic cups
- 1 cup per person for washing (lemon wedge).
- 1 cup per person for dipping (parsley).
  Pour a dash of salt in each cup.

DAY OF PASSOVER:

- Remove all leaven/yeast products (as best as possible).
- Lightly dust
- Roast lamb - refer to "Menu" sheet.
- Boil/roast eggs - refer to "Menu" sheet for recipe - #5
- Make Charoset - refer to "Menu" sheet for recipe - #1
- Wash/cut lemons into thin ½ slices for drinking (optional). Cut thin ¼ wedges for hand washing. Store in sandwich bag, refrigerate.
- Wash/cut parsley - 1 sprig per person. Store in sandwich bag, refrigerate.
- Include large sprigs for the number of Seder plates (2-3).
- Set aside 3 whole sheets of Matzoh bread, put into Matzoh Tosh bag.
- Break up Matzoh in pieces. 1 sheet per plate. Set on table.
- Hide breadcrumbs (Leaven): Limit to one room. Make it easy to find.
- Fill teakettle with water.
- Keep kitchen clean and clutter free. Wash dirty dishes, pots & pans immediately after using them.

1½ Hour Before Guests Arrive: (4:00pm)

- Get dressed. Hostess wear apron to keep dress clean.
- Fill drinking glasses with water. Put a lemon slice on rim of glass (optional).
- Fill small cups on tray
    - 1st set: 1 sprig of parsley per cup, add water
    - 2nd set: ¼ lemon wedge per cup, add water
    - Set at each place setting
- Candy/Nut cups (optional)
    - Set at each place setting.
- Cut up meat
    - Cut out shank bone and keep for next year (optional).
    - Transfer meat to a 9 x 13 pan.
    - Add small amount of meat juice in pan, cover with foil and keep warm in oven at 170 degrees.
- Make gravy - Pour ¾ of the meat juice through strainer into a medium saucepan, add flour and browning sauce. Add salt/pepper to taste.
- Make up Seder Plate(s)
    - Charoset
    - Shank Bones
    - Whole eggs
    - Maror (horseradish)
    - Parsley
    - Onions
    - Set plates out on table.
- Heat soup through, keep on simmer (delegate to stir).
- Set out hot fudge.
- Open and set bottles of sparkling grape juice/wine on table.
- Put ice cubes in drinking glasses, use tongs (delegate).
- Fill pitchers with ice and put on table.
- Light candles, but leave one unlit (for the blessing).
- Fill large washbowl with warm water.
- Set egg plates on Food Table.
- Have an empty garbage bag or wastebasket ready after the meal to scrape off left over food. Throw out all plastic ware and paper products.
- Host & Hostess put head coverings on.

פֶסַח SAMPLE PASSOVER SCHEDULE

When People Arrive:
- Have husband greet guests and take coats (if any).
- Cold foods go in refrigerator until ready to serve.
- Warm foods go in low heat oven 170 degrees until ready to serve.

Start Passover:
- Have the head of the household find crumbs using feather and linen napkin.
- Everyone find a seat around the dining room table.
- To make things move faster, delegate help in serving.

For Dinner:
- Serve soup first - delegate 2 people to ladle soup. Set on tray and serve.
- While soup is being served...
    - Heat water for decaf tea, add (2) tea bags (Hostess).
    - Transfer lamb to platter & serve (Hostess).
    - Heat gravy through & serve (Hostess).
    - Delegate help to bring food out to the food table.
    - Scrape/soak/stack dishes immediately after the meal (Hostess).

For Dessert:
- Warm hot fudge & get strawberries (Hostess). Put toppings on table.
- Delegate 2 people to cut up cake & scoop ice cream. Set on tray & serve.
- Delegate a person to serve tea & refill water pitchers.
- Clear Food Table & put away left over food while dessert is being served (Hostess).

After the Celebration:
- Collect all paper/plastic waste in a trash bag.
- Put away any left over dessert/food (Hostess).
- When guests are ready to leave, give back dishes, chairs, and any food that is left over that was brought.
- Keep name place cards after the party for next year.
- Keep Haggadahs, song sheets, and song tape for next year.

Jesus said to them, "With fervent desire
I have desired to eat this Passover
with you before I suffer."
                Luke 22:15

He restores my soul;
He leads me in the paths of righteousness
for His name's sake.
                Psalm 23:3

Who may ascend into the Hill of the Lord?
Or who may stand in His holy place?
He who has clean hands
and a pure heart. . .
                Psalm 24: 3,4

Lift up your heads, O you gates!
And be lifted up, you everlasting doors!
And the King of glory shall come in.
                Psalm 24:7

In Him was life, and the life was the light of men.
And the light shines in the darkness,
and the darkness did not comprehend it.
                John 1:5

And the Word became flesh and dwelt among us,
and we beheld His glory,
the glory as of the only begotten of the Father,
full of grace and truth.
                John 1:14

Behold! The Lamb of God
who takes away
the sin of the world!
                John 1:29

פֶּסַח SAMPLE VERSES FOR THE PASSOVER TABLE

For God so loved the world
that He gave His only begotten Son,
 that whoever believes in Him
should not perish but have everlasting life.
John 3:16

"I am the bread of life.
He who comes to Me shall never hunger,
 and he who believes in Me
 shall never thirst."
John 6:35

"I am the light of the world.
He who follows Me shall not walk in darkness,
but have the light of life."
John 8:12

"I am the Good Shepherd.
The Good shepherd
gives his life for the sheep."
John 10:11

"I am the resurrection and the life.
He who believes in Me though he may die,
shall live."
John 11:25

"I am the way, the truth, and the life.
 No one come to the Father
 except through Me."
John 14:6

"I go and prepare a place for you,
I will come again and receive you to Myself;
that where I am,
there you may be also."
John 14:3

"In the world you will have tribulation;
but be of good cheer,
I have overcome the world."
John 16:33

"And this is eternal life,
that they may know You,
the only true God, and Jesus Christ
whom You have sent."
John 17:3

פֶּסַח CHILDREN AND THE PASSOVER

Contributed by Mrs. Julie Renzema

When my husband and I began celebrating Passover seven years ago we joined another Christian family to celebrate. Three years later we decided to go on our own and celebrate our first Passover at home. Accustomed to a smooth flow of liturgy - meal - liturgy, we were taken a little off guard that first year at the length of time it took to complete our celebration (4+ hours)! The reason for the excessive length was that we had not accounted for the need to quiet and entertain a 2 year old during the meal. Nor had we figured on having an 'intermission' after the meal to put our daughter to bed. The next year flowed a bit better, as I prepared a few toys ahead of time, and delegated some of the jobs during our intermission. Now, our Passover runs much smoother and is enjoyed by everyone, regardless of age.

Having the whole family be part of the Passover celebration is crucial—there is such a unity that comes from being together and remembering what Christ has done for us over the ages. It is a legacy to be told and shared with even the smallest ones. Our children are now 5, 4, 3, 2, and 3 months and I enjoy having them join me in preparing for our Passover Celebration. Their ages force me to be a bit creative and flexible so that they can be actively involved in the preparations and liturgy for the evening.

I used Mrs. Greenfield's Sample Preparation Schedule (page 76) as my baseline, in order to decrease any unwanted stress on the day of our Seder. I have modified the schedule to reflect having my children involved in the preparations. The following changes have been made to accommodate the ages of our children.

פסח CHILDREN AND THE PASSOVER

Passover Minus 5 Days:
· Get out Passover box and check the supply of 5 oz. clear plastic glasses, 9 oz. clear plastic cups (goblets), 10 oz. clear plastic soup bowls, and paper dinner napkins.
· Get out Passover books to read to the children.
· Get out table cloth(s) – press and hang.
· Make Grocery List for the week.

Minus 4 Days:
· Make ice cubes
· Read introductory Passover story to the children.
· Check supply of crayons and purchase small boxes of crayons from the dollar store for each child's place or divide current supply of crayons into Ziploc snack bags for each child's place (set aside).
· Begin teaching children the "4 Questions."
   1. Why is this night different from all other nights? On other nights we eat the leavened or the unleavened bread. Why on this night only the matzoh – the unleavened bread?
   2. On all other nights we eat any kind of vegetables. Why on this night only maror – the bitter herbs?
   3. On all other nights we are not required to dip our vegetables even once. Why on this night two times?
   4. On all other nights we eat sitting upright or reclining. Why on this night do all recline?

Tradition has it that the youngest child asks the four questions. However, due to the ages of my children I distribute the questions amongst them based on ability.

Minus 3 Days:
· Put together the children's haggadahs.
· Make enough copies for our family and any additional children.
· Make the place cards for the Passover table with the children.
· Read another Passover story.
· Work on "4 Questions."

פֶּסַח CHILDREN AND THE PASSOVER

Minus 2 Days:
· Make-Ahead Mash Potatoes - Have the children use kids knives and cut potatoes, help mash, measure ingredients, and stir.
· Read another Passover story.
· Talk about cleaning the house for any signs of "chametz" = sin and how the Jews burn the chametz, but Jesus has taken our "chametz" away when He died on the cross, so we don't have to burn the leaven food but instead set it outside to reminded us of what Jesus has done.
· Work on "4 Questions."

Minus 1 Day:
· Cut parsley and lemons – put in Ziploc bags.
· Make charoset with the children.
· Read another Passover story – talk about Elijah and Jesus coming again.
· Work on "4 Questions."
· After children go to bed:Set serving dishes and place settings on the counter (out of reach).
Set table decorations on counter – hang banners
Set up tables and chairs
· I make nut cups rather than party favors so the kids aren't distracted too much from the celebration, yet they have something to munch on before the meal is served.

PASSOVER:
Review the "4 Questions" throughout the day.

In the morning:
Make Roasted eggs- have the children help peel the shells off.
Break up the matzoh bread – we do this in Ziploc bags – the children love it!

After lunch:
Have husband take kids out to the park, so I can set the table and finish decorations. Layout children's haggadah's and make sure crayons are within reach.

פֶּסַח CHILDREN AND THE PASSOVER

Older children can help put together the sedar plates.
We usually have 2.

1 ½ hour before guests come:
Mom gets dressed
Set out the children's clothes
Dress the baby
Dad gets dressed and supervises children dressing

After the Meal:
· Delegate guests to help with scraping/stacking dishes, picking up garbage, and putting food away.
· Change baby and younger children into pajamas.
· Sing a few worship songs with group, then put youngest children to bed.
· Complete the liturgy.

Family Passover Preparations:
As my children have gotten older, preparing for Passover has become a family activity. I really try to make the preparations as inviting as possible to the children by displaying my own excitement and enthusiasm for the event. Below is a list of the preparations I make a point of including the children in to help them take ownership of the celebration.

1. Making ice cubes for our guests.
2. Cleaning our rooms
    a. Talk about what the Israelites houses were like and what they were able to take from their homes when they left Egypt.
    b. Talk about the chametz (sin), and how our hearts are able to be cleaned by Jesus by His dying on the cross.
3. Preparing the potatoes
    a. Washing the potatoes
    b. Cutting them with a children's knife
    c. Mashing the potatoes with a hand masher
    d. Measuring ingredients for the recipe

4. Preparing the soup
   a. Handing me ingredients to cut
   b. Putting ingredients in the pot.

5. Washing parsley, lemons, and apples

6. Breaking off pieces of parsley and putting in Ziploc bag

7. Placing cut lemons in Ziploc bag

8. Making charoset – I have an enclosed hand chopper and the children use this to dice the apples and nuts. We then take turns putting the ingredients in the bowl and stirring the mixture. Of course everyone gets a taste-test of their work.

9. Breaking the matzoh into pieces - Make sure and talk about why we eat the matzoh, why we don't break 6 of the matzoh up, and where the matzoh are placed during the celebration (matza tosh bag).

10. Preparing the roasted eggs
   a. After the hard-boiled eggs have cooled, letting the children help me shell the eggs.
   b. Poking them with a safety pin (with my assistance)
   c. Placing on the baking pan

Spiritual Preparations:

Throughout the week I look for opportunities to talk about Passover. I use the preparations as opportunities to share how our history is related to the Israelites, and how Jesus has made it possible to celebrate this event. I use a lot of Bible stories and Passover books to explain: the liturgy of the evening, the Seder plate, and the foods that are used in the meal, the history of the Israelites, Moses, and Jesus. I give my children a lot of details, some they remember, some they don't (some they surprise me with 3 + months after Passover).

The follow is a list of resources I use to prepare myself to share with my children during the Passover week.

פסח INTERNET RESOURCES

www.torahtots.com/holidays/pesach/pesach.htm
This website is wonderful !!

www.kidsdomain.com/holiday/passover
This site covers what is Passover, printables: coloring pages, mazes, and word puzzles, crafts, links to other Passover sites.

http://scheinerman.net/judaism/pesach/index.html
A great website for familiarizing yourself with Passover and activities for families with young children. This site includes a Passover haggadah for Jewish families with young children and a bibliography of more books to read to children about Passover.

www.hanukat.com
Select "stories," and this will get you to a "treasure hunt" game to foster the retrieval of the affikomen.

http://www.bry-backmanor.org
This is a great resource for many holidays and seasons. Select holidays to explore Passover or Activities for printable sheets.

www.billybear4kids.com
Scroll down and select "Holidays", on the next screen, scroll down, and select "Pesach" then you will find the mazes.

www.makingfriends.com/redsea.htm
Fun craft activity you can do before Passover feast, and children can play with during the litergury.

http://www.holidays.net/passover/
General information about Passover and recipes.

פסח BOOKS TO READ TO CHILDREN

Pearl's Passover: A Family Celebration through stories, recipes, crafts, and songs by Jane Breskin Zalben - This book is full of neat ideas for young children to utilize in preparing for Passover tucked into neat stories. My children really liked this one.

Passover by June Behrens

What is Passover? By Harriet Ziefert - a lift the flap book

Ask Another Question by Miriam Chaikin

A Picture Book of PASSOVER by David A. Adler

On Passover by Cathy Goldberg Fishman

Matzo Ball Moon by Leslea Newman

Matzoh Mouse by Lauren L. Wohl

The Story of Passover by Norma Simon

Passover Magic by Roni Schotter

Passover by Miriam Nerlove

The Wineglass A Passover Story by Norman Rosten

The Story of Passover by Bobbi Katz

The Matzah That Papa Brought Home by Fran Manushkin

Passover by Norma Simon

פסח THE HAGGADAH FOR CHILDREN

My final act of including my children in the liturgy of the evening is to make a haggadah for them. I utilize the above internet resources and the idea books to create a haggadah in a coloring book format to help the children follow along through the evening.

I found a picture of a family celebrating Passover at www.kids-domain.com/holiday/passover/color/plate9.gif and used it to create a title page.

Next I went to www.torahtots.com/holidays/pesach/bedika.htm to get coloring pictures of searching for the chametz, burning chametz, the sedar plate, blessing the meal, washing the hands, eating the greens (karpas), breaking the matzoh, recounting the exodus story, Moses, the plagues, eating the elements, retrieving the afikomn, Elijah's place, and songs of praise.

I then went to www.kidsdomain.com and selected a maze to the chametz and one to the afikomen (www.billybear4kids.com also has a chametz maze). I also included a neat activity sheet from www.bry-backmanor.org called "Find the Chametz." At www.billybear4kids.com I found a mazes of baby Moses and the basket and the Israelites crossing the Red Sea. I found a picture of a drawing of a group of children in and then I added the "4 Questions" beneath it with my word processing program.

The Jewish haggadahs end with the fourth cup of praise not yet complete. I found that the resources would use a coloring picture of a goat or lamb to be sacrificed again next year until God brings freedom to all. Since we believe that Jesus is the lamb that was sacrificed for our redemption and given us freedom I have chosen to place a picture of Him at the end of the children's coloring book. The final page of the book is a picture with the wine glass, grapes, and Jewish star – and the words "Next Year in the NEW JERUSALEM".

פסח THE HAGGADAH FOR CHILDREN

I used a simple word processing program to make titles of the points in the liturgy and placed them under the coloring pictures, so my children would recognize the key words to follow along with the adult haggadahs.

After completing my original copy, I take it to the local copy store and make enough copies for my children and any guests. Then I place the haggadahs in ½ inch 3 ring binders. I tried the paper 3 prong folders the first year – but one spill of water resulted in a teal blue stained tablecloth. Each year I add or subtract pictures as the children mature.

As my kids mature, I plan to modify the haggadahs to reflect their maturity and understanding. At http://www.torahtots.com/holidays/pesach/pesach.htm under the "Fun & Games" heading, I found some neat puzzles, more complicated mazes, word searches, secret codes, and pickle puzzles.

I would encourage you to celebrate Passover, and especially to celebrate with your children. It is a family time meant for all ages. Jesus Himself said, " Let the little children come to me." What a wonderful way to show your children that the children of Israel are now our brothers and sisters as we have been grafted into the vine through Jesus Christ. It is through Him that we can partake of this wonderful event.

Printed in the USA
CPSIA information can be obtained
at www.ICGtesting.com
JSHW020458180324
59338JS00002B/98